LISTEN AND LOOK!
A Safety Book

By Rita Golden Gelman   Illustrated by Cathy Beylon

LISTEN AND LOOK
A Safety Book

If you were a goat,
You could open your throat

And swallow a shirt or a shell.
Then you could look
For a shoe or a book
And eat them for dinner as well.

But if you are human,

You have to take care,
Whether you live North or South.
You have to eat food
that is thoroughly chewed and...

Don't put strange things in your mouth!

It's okay for noodles,
And cheese,
And tomatoes.
For orange juice, lettuce,
Leftover potatoes,
Spaghetti,
Salami,
Pastrami and ham,
Tuna fish salad
And strawberry jam,
Hamburgers,
Sandwiches,
Cantaloupes too.

It's okay for them,

But NEVER for you!

A collie I know
Loves the ice and the snow.
And she doesn't need boots on her feet.

It would be most absurd
To catch sight of a bird
In a raincoat and hat on the street.

When it's windy and cold,
Or so I am told,
The elephants walk around bare.

But people get sickly in cold pretty quickly.
They have to watch out what they wear.

For a parrot it's easy.
An elephant too.
And a monkey can do stuff
That people can't do.

A giraffe has no problems.
Nor does a horse.
And gorillas are bigger than you are,
Of course.

So if something important
Is on the top shelf,

Ask for it.
Don't try to get it yourself.

A butterfly crosses the street in the air.
So do a pigeon and crow.

A mole doesn't worry.
He's not in a hurry.
He crosses the street from below.

An elephant does it
  wherever she wants.
She's so big and so fat
  and so tall.

A fish doesn't care
If the traffic is there.
He doesn't do it at all.

But you and your friends,
You're not big.
You're not fat.
And *you* have to walk with your feet.
You haven't got wings
Or burrowing things,

So LOOK when you're crossing the street.

BOTH WAYS.

Sometimes you're flying a rocket.
Sometimes you're racing a car.
Sometimes you're with
   an invisible friend
And you really don't care where you are.

But whether you're riding or rowing,
Or crawling or climbing a tree,

Look where you're going or you could end up
In a place where you don't want to be!

When a turtle says no
he hides in his shell.

An ostrich can kick
and she does it quite well.

A squid can squirt.
A quill can hurt.

A worm can wiggle away in the dirt.

A bear can say no with his
teeth and his paws.

A crab can say no with her
jaggedy claws.

A burro can bray it.

A skunk can spray it.
The only way *you* can say no is to...

SAY IT!

The End